GOD WILL RIGHT YOUR WRONG

Compiled by
DR.NATASHA BIBBINS

God Will Right Your Wrong
Copyright © March 2023
Compiled by Dr. Natasha Bibbins
Published in the United States of America by
ChosenButterflyPublishing LLC

ChosenButterfly
Publishing

www.cb-publishing.com

ISBN: 978-1-945377-28-0

Printed in the United States of America

March 2023

Table of Contents:

Foreword

I believe that this read is going to help to assist you on your journey to build and advance. My experience with building and advancement hasn't always been easy; however, it's worth sharing with everyone. One of the things I had to accept was I had to stop waiting for others to have control of my situation. I made a choice to take authority and use it to my advantage. I had to participate in my deliverance, also my freedom. When I made a better decision, I began to see better results, so my recommendation to you is to change what you don't like about yourself and your circumstances and move towards expecting better results.

My first step was to identify what needed to be changed in my life. I no longer enjoyed the pleasures of drugs; I didn't like the road of addiction anymore. I made a choice to get off that road; however, although I wanted to let go of those toxic moments, it didn't want to let me go. I was stuck with the reality of the road I was on and the destination I was going to end up at—either prison or dead. I began to pray and ask the intercessors to go to God on my behalf, so what I didn't have the ability to do for myself others might be willing to help me with. God heard my prayers and their prayers in addition to me participating in my deliverance and it's still working to this day. I believe this book is going to rescue you from similar challenges and prevent you from becoming a repeat offender. So, let's move into the place where we're open to ask for help and add help as it is needed. Let's go and God Bless!

Pastor Lonney Davis

Participating in Your Deliverance

―――――――⸎⸎―――――――

Pastor Lonney Davis

"And if it seems evil unto you to serve the Lord, choose you this day whom ye will serve whether the gods which your fathers served that were on the other side of the flood or the gods of the Amorites in whose land ye dwell but as for me and my house we will serve the Lord."

Many people in the body of Christ are of the mindset that God is going to do this thing for me when He gets ready. How many of us have heard this statement before? Please allow me to be of assistance to you by saying that you must be willing to give God access to the areas where you need Him to deliver you. A lot of times we manufacture weak excuses to justify staying in the pits of our bondage because it is a place we have grown accustomed to being in. Simply put, many of us have normalized bondage.

Consider this: have you ever been in a situation where someone borrowed money from you and you were never repaid? It's an uncomfortable position to be in. You may feel like you've been taken advantage of by the person; you may let it slide for a while; however, when you finally get the courage or when your patience runs out, you ask the person, "When are you going to be able to pay me back?"

The other person replies in a high-pitched voice, "I didn't pay you back? I forgot all about that." Well, just because they may have forgotten that doesn't mean the debt shouldn't be paid.

Understand that, just as the person may have forgotten that debt over time, you too can be in bondage so long as you forget that freedom is an option. You will begin to justify and normalize the state you're in simply because of how long you have been in that place. The Bible declares, "There is a way that seemeth right unto a man, but the end thereof are the ways of death." Proverbs 14:12

Have you ever been in that place, that place where you became accustomed to dysfunction and bondage? Over the course of time you may have asked, "How did I get here?" And trust me; we've all been there and I don't point my finger at you for getting into this storm.

My suggestion is this: don't be like the man who has money but lacks the wisdom to invest his money in such a way as to bring a greater profit. What does that man do? He invests his money in property that has no value and there is no growth. In addition to that aspect there are no potential tenants because of the condition of the property and then he realizes he's made a poor decision.

I want you to understand that you don't have to respond to every invite or temptation. I must be honest with you; I have never been in a social club in my life, but I know people who have been in these kinds of places. I would often ask them what goes on inside and there seemed to be overall consensus that, "We just sit around and socialize and may have a drink and once in a while get up and dance."

I would ask my friends, "Is that's all you go for?" I expressed to those friends that it made no sense at all. Why would I get dressed up to go to a social club and not get engaged and just sit there like a wallflower? If you go to a party you might start a conversation leading up to other things such as dancing and drinking, which might lead to other activities.

The key to participating in your own deliverance is you must start by telling your flesh, "I am not going down the path of bondage anymore." In the text, Joshua says, "If you think that it is evil to serve the Lord, then go back to your fathers, go back to the place before the flood." Some of us come from situations that were so bad that we were messed up in the first place. Let me speak about me; first and foremost, God made it so bad for me that I couldn't go back.

"Go back to your father's place." This begins to speak the truth to us; because of our human nature, our sin nature, we are quick to retract and go back to the things we are familiar with. The enemy wants you to go back and find some level of comfort in that bondage. Joshua tells the Israelites to go ahead and go back to their fathers. He goes on to say, "as for me and my house we will serve the Lord."

Please take note that the house in this verse consists of walls, a structured building and a place where we dwell. I want to add that house in this text is also the temple of your body. Notice Joshua said, "me and my house." I want to encourage you that God will make a way of escape for you. That is the amazing thing about God; He places responsibility upon Himself for holding us up and sustaining us until He allows us to achieve the revelation out of what we are going through. I must say that it might not be easy, but God will reward you in this effort. I absolutely believe that true deliverance comes when you can stand on your testimony.

Be encouraged and keep striving.

Participate in your deliverance.

Pastor Lonney Davis

Lonney Davis is the Founder of the Faith in God Anointed Ministry.

Pastor Davis is an innovative executive with a strong lead role calling in ministry, recognized for utilizing his team-building abilities & business experiences to positively impact the Church of the Lord Jesus Christ & the faith-based non-profit community, by strategically capitalizing on an organization's strengths and minimizing its weaknesses, thus allowing these spiritually driven entities to naturally thrive, so that the Kingdom of God can be advanced and expanded.

Pastor Lonney L.Davis Sr. is a devoted husband to Sis. Tamra D. Davis they have 7 wonderful children. He is a family man and have strong deep roots in raising his family in the admonition of the Lord.

Before serving as Pastor, He worked well with Pastor Joseph Kyles as his adjutant. Pastor Davis was ordained as a Elder in the COGIC in 2004 by Ordination Board of Elders in the COGIC organization headed by Pastor M.Bowen under the leadership of Bishop Cody Marshall.

Pastor Lonney Davis Sr. continues to serve on the Pastors' Board as the Treasurer and many other Auxillaries. Pastor Lonney Davis Sr. is dedicated and have a passion to public service and spiritual empowering through Biblical principles in our local communities. Pastor Davis has been a well sought after television and radio host and now presently is on the web spreading the Gospel and educating people about the needed and necessary changes that are possible in our lives.

Contact Information:

Facebook: Lonney Davis
Clubhouse: Lonney Davis
YouTube: Pastor Lonney Davis
Website: www.lonneydavis.com
Email: prophetldavis@yahoo.com

Bruised, Broken and now Better

Denise Watson-Smith

Synopsis:

Sometimes, life will throw some things our way that we have not bargained for. We are not often ready for the pain, especially when it is self-inflicted. This chapter covers a period in my life where I messed up trying to help a friend in need and found myself locked up. Guilt, shame and self-condemnation were my story. I experienced hurt from those I thought would love me in the midst of the mess and received condemnation from them. I was angry with myself and wanted to die. I was convinced that God did not love me and surely He would not want to use me. I was a disappointment to myself and to others and could not fathom anyone loving me. Everything that went wrong in my marriage I blamed on me. I stopped loving me because I allowed myself to feel instead of think. I did not use wisdom, nor did I pray when I helped a friend out of a situation. I just had this notion that I was called to help! My helping hurt me and caused me to be bruised and broken … but, somehow, along the way, I started to become better!

Life has a way of creeping up on you, right when you least expect it. One minute you feel as if you are doing everything right and the next thing, you find out that right goes completely out of the window. Sometimes you let your heart get in the way of logic and you find yourself sitting behind bars trying to figure life out. For me, I allowed my own desire to help everyone cause me to hurt everyone.

I allowed myself to break the law in order to help a friend, but the price of helping a friend got me 15 weekends in jail and eight months wearing a home electronic device. I was devastated; I hid what I had done from my family, from my husband, until a few days before I was to go report for my first weekend. I was angry, hurt and ashamed. I was so busy being busy that I lost sight of everyone and everything else that mattered. My mind said I was doing a good thing, but I knew it was not the right thing.

I felt like I had brought shame to my husband and children and I wanted to die. I was thinking of ways to take my own life, but I was also too afraid to have my family find me; they were already disappointed in me, and I was disappointed in myself. I remember the look on my husbands' face that first weekend; he looked utterly ashamed, and he reminded me that I could have caused him to lose his position at work. This was not the happiest time for us; I felt guilty, he felt disappointed, and I had no idea if we were going to make it.

During this time, I had met a beautiful young woman who went to summer school at UVA; she was mentored by my goddaughter, and she had such a beautiful spirit. The anointing on her life was amazing, but she doubted herself so much. In between weekends, I got to know this precious one until one day she came to our home, and she was so upset. She sat down and talked to me and said these words: "There is so much that God is showing me, and I am afraid that if I tell what God is saying, they will not listen to me because I am so young." I remember telling her that she had an obligation to tell whomever what God said, and if they did not listen, it was not on her. I told her that she was God's mouthpiece and she just must tell them what He said.

She then looked at me and said these words: "Momma, God said that if you don't do what you are called to do, you will die on the operating table." There I was doing weekends in jail and then being told that if I did not do what I was called to do, I was going to die. My Lord, I was not ready for that word, and I will admit I was a little speculative since I'd had no one tell me that I was going to have surgery.

Two weeks after she spoke those words, I had my annual exam. Within the next two days I received a phone call stating that they were sending me to a specialist due to some abnormalities they found. An appointment was scheduled for me, and I went in for it. After that appointment, I was informed that my uterus and my ovaries were enlarged and I was going to have to have a complete hysterectomy; but all I heard was, "If you don't do what you are called to do, you are going to die on the operating table." I was afraid; there I was, spending weekends in jail and running from whom God called me to be. Parts of me felt as if I got in trouble in order to keep Him from using me. I had a plan for my life, but my plan was not God's plan.

My surgery was scheduled to take place in two weeks, and I had not finished my weekends. I remember having to petition to have my weekends put on hold temporarily so I could have my surgery. My last weekend in jail before my surgery was that of August 13th, 2004, with my surgery being scheduled for the 16th, which was on a Monday. I went in for my weekend at 7:00 p.m. on that Friday.

During the night, when everyone was sleeping, we heard glass breaking from upstairs; the male inmates upstairs were holding a deputy hostage after they had beat him. They took his keys and began to run loose through the jail. The deputy they beat was an older gentleman and I remember that they called in the city, county and state police and the jail was placed on lockdown status. The female deputy came into the area where I was (the work release area, which is where they put the weekenders) on that Saturday and stated that if the lockdown was not lifted, I might not be able to leave at my scheduled time on Sunday, which was the 15th, the day before my surgery. They had not recaptured all of the male inmates that were running lose in the jailhouse, but before 7:00 p.m. on that Saturday, they had them all back in custody and the male deputy was transported to the hospital.

I got home on that Sunday evening and got the call for the exact time my surgery was scheduled. My husband and I left Monday morning to go to the hospital for my surgery; I remember my surgeon saying there would be a pathologist in the operating room to slice my ovaries and my uterus once they were removed to check for cancer. She stated that if it turned out to be cancerous, they would have to cut me vertically to as opposed to horizontally. I went in for surgery and when I woke up in the recovery room, I felt my stomach first to see where my bandages were placed, and I knew that it was not cancerous.

I guess one can see that life was still happening; I stayed in the hospital until that Thursday and then I was discharged. I spent the next few days recuperating and I told myself that I would go back to finish up my last weekend that following Friday. I still heard those words though, "God said that you were going to die on the operating table if you don't do what you are called to do." The following Friday, I stayed in bed and rested, knowing that I was going in to finish up my last weekend at 7:00 p.m. that night.

Around 1:00 p.m., I started getting sick in my stomach; the pain started out dull, but it intensified until I had to be taken to the emergency room thinking that this was a result of the surgery. When I was called back to see the physician, a series of tests was run only for me to discover that I had a partial bowel obstruction and they admitted me. The next day, the surgeon came in and stated that they were not going to operate because I also had an enlarged gall bladder with numerous gall stones and that was a game changer. I remained in the hospital an extra week before being sent home and being sent to see a gastroenterologist. Once I started seeing the gastroenterologist, it was determined that I would have to have yet another surgery. I just knew that God had a sense of humor. I was tired, lost, confused, still ashamed and still knew that my family was disappointed because I had failed them.

My gallbladder surgery was scheduled for November 1st; it was outpatient, so I came home right afterwards. My life was changing, yet I was still hurting. I had not been to church due to the weekends, and I did not want to go to church because of the meanness of some that I went to church with. I had messed up, not in church, but I was tried and convicted in church. Romans 8:1 reminded me that there was no condemnation for those who are in Christ Jesus, but I found myself being condemned ... in church. I wanted so much to still be loved in church, but I felt distant and isolated.

My weekends were placed on hold until February 2005. Because they were put on hold, I went back to church, but it was hard. During that time, I started to really seek God for myself, and I started going to a school of ministry with another church during the week. That church was so inviting and warm, but I knew that I could not leave my church because God did not say so. God had a plan; I just did not see it.

January came, then February, and I went back to jail to finish what I thought was my last weekend, only to find out that I would have to complete two more weekends, one full weekend and the next weekend was just one full 24-hour day. After that last weekend, I was supposed to go immediately into home monitoring, but, for some reason, I slipped through the cracks and was released without the home monitoring.

Life was still happening, and I was still hurting. I felt like the woman caught in adultery in the Bible because of the ridicule. I still went to church, but I was seeking God for myself outside of church. During that time, God put some amazing people in my life to encourage me and to push me, but during July of 2005, I discovered that I had a tear in my meniscus and a tumor; there I was getting ready to have another surgery.

My surgery was scheduled for July of that year and after the surgery, I get a subpoena from the court to appear.

They finally caught back up with me and it was time for me to get my home monitoring device and spend the next eight months on lockdown. My eight months on home monitoring began in August, 2005.

During those eight months was when the actual hell began. My husband, though he loved me, was still disappointed in me; I was an embarrassment to him, and rightfully so. I was unable to attend any functions, I was not the ideal wife; I WAS TROUBLE and I brought shame to him. I became so angry with myself that I thought about dying again at my own hands. My family did not deserve the shame and embarrassment that I put them through. And it appeared that some people in my church became even meaner.

I was on home monitoring for a month before I was allowed to go to church on Sundays. That first Sunday back in church with the bracelet around my ankle, I pulled into the parking lot and sat in the car until I got the nerve to get out. My husband had duty that weekend as an Active Guard Reservist, so I had to face the ridicule on my own. I finally got out of the car and was greeted by one of the deacons in church who always was an advocate of mine and I felt much better for seeing a friend.

When I arrived inside the building, it was a different story. I went in and sat down; my best friend arrived shortly afterwards and sat with me. I sat in the middle of the pew of the church, and I was talking to my best friend when I looked up and saw a deaconess walking up the aisle; she looked over at me and blurted out, "I thought you were locked up!"

The look on my face must have been one of brokenness my best friend looked at me and said, "It's going to be alright." I was so angry and even more ashamed because there were people there who did not know me and were sitting in my proximity; they must have heard her because they were sitting in front of me and to the left of me. I turned and looked behind me and there was my husband, sitting a few rows behind me. I looked at him and I felt two things— he was there as a support but also sitting away from me because he was ashamed. I wanted to crawl under a rock and never come out. I could not wait for church to end that day and when I walked out to my car to leave, one of the trustees of the church pulled his vehicle up and looked down at my leg while asking me if I had seen his sister-in-law. I was so humiliated, but I grew even angrier at myself. I felt like I was nothing and really did not want to go on.

Things even became more strained between me and my husband. I know he loved me, but he became fixated on a woman from our church; he was "encouraged" to participate in a study that she was conducting, and they forged a friendship that was more of an unholy alliance. He was sneaking to call her, and she was calling him in private. He started acting very suspiciously, and all the signs were there that my husband was having an emotional and intimate affair with this woman. He would talk to her before talking to me. When I realized this, I was devasted and I felt defeated. Why? Because had it not been for me getting into trouble, I could have been the woman he married and not the one that caused him shame and embarrassment. I could not be who he needed me to be and that was all on me.

During that time, my mother-in-law passed away and I was unable to be who he needed me to be. I could not go with him when he had to go to the nursing home after her passing, nor was I able to go with him home to West Virginia for her funeral. He did not call and talk to me on the highway when he got the call that she had passed; he called to talk to his friend. He was hurting and I was not helping him; I was a hindrance. My heart was crushed, all he needed was his wife's support and yet I could not offer him what he needed; at least, I did not think I could.

I was so eaten up with guilt that I could no longer see the good in me and I was completely broken. It was then that I could hear God say, "NOW I CAN USE YOU!" I decided at that moment to go into the enemy's camp and take back EVERYTHING that he had stolen from me, right down to the things that I appeared to be giving up. I wanted my life back! It was at that moment that I gave God a yes! It was at that moment that I realized that, though I had got myself into trouble, God was there with me and it was all part of

His plan to get me back to that place in Him for me to walk in the anointing and calling that He had on my life. He did not kill me on the operating table, but I was slowly dying running still from the yes!

My yes to my calling began not only to heal me, but it also allowed others to be free because they could see the same God that delivered and set me free was the same God that would do the same for them. I felt like Leah, trying to do everything to make my husband see me and still needing to know if he loved me and forgave me for being such a failure but then moving to a place of praising God during it all. I took my eyes off him, my husband, and put them on Him, God! I was walking in utter devastation, feeling deserted by my husband because I embarrassed him, but holding up my head and knowing that God loved me, and He had forgiven me. I began to walk with God in a way that I never had before and then I began to see that even during the mess I made, God still favored me. I found favor with God and with man, but I had to stop walking in pity and start trusting God with it all.

In April 2006, the lieutenant and the corporal in the city jail came to my home and parked around the back under my carport as they always did to remove the home monitoring device. We had coffee together and the corporal reminded me, "We always saw something special in you, and that is why we made the promise to you that we will never cause you any embarrassment. That is why we would never park in the front of your house." What I did not see before I saw then, God's favor.

Throughout this whole ordeal, I wanted to leave my church, but God would not allow it; I went to my pastor two weeks after I came off home monitoring and said to him that God had called me to preach. He talked to me for a while and inquired of me when I knew. I shared with him that I had always known, but I did not want to answer God's call. My pastor then looked at me and said, "What if I don't allow you to go forth, what then?"

To this I replied, "Pastor, my life is not worth living if I can't do the thing that God has called me to do!"

One year later, God allowed me to go forth and render my initial sermon, and four years later, He blessed me to be ordained in that same place. I have always been told, "Don't outrun your interference!" God had a plan, and I wanted to run! I tried to leave the place where I was hurt before God released me; BUT GOD.

Author Denise Watson-Smith

Denise is the visionary and founder of Weapons of Praise and Becoming You Christian Life Coaching and the co-owner of Inspired Scribe Publishers. Denise is a licensed and ordained minister of the Gospel with a tremendous passion for writing. She was born and raised in Roanoke, Virginia; a 1985 graduate of William Fleming High School and 1988 graduate of Virginia Western Community College with an Associate Degree in Criminal Justice. She later went back to school to obtain her Bachelor's in Religious Studies at Liberty University and her MDiv. from Liberty Theological Seminary with a concentration in Pastoral Studies. Denise is currently enrolled at Regent University in the Doctoral Program for strategic leadership.

Denise met and married the love of her life, Victor Smith (retired Army Sgt.), in 1995. Together, they have four amazing children: Wesley, JeTashawna, Victoria and Victor II. She has two beautiful daughters-in-law, TaLesia Smith, married to Victor, and Prentice Brown, who was married to Wesley. Denise also has ten beautiful grandchildren: Neveah, TiYani, Rylan, MaKayla, Ariyann, LeiAni, Kaden, Elijah, Cairo and Journii. Denise and her husband attend the Impact Worship Center International under the leadership of Rev. Dr. Brennetta Williams. Denise and her husband reside in Suffolk, Va.

Contact Information:

Email: denisewatson.smith@icloud.com
Facebook: https://www.facebook.com/dwatsonsmith
Facebook: https://www.facebook.com/beaccountabletoyou
Facebook:https://www.facebook.com/weaponsofpraise2015
Instagram: https://instagram.com/weaponsofpraise
Instagram: https://instagram.com/becomingyouclc

Denise's Acknowledgments:

To my husband Victor, for loving me and never giving up on me.

To my children for just being who you are.

To my friend, Adrienne, thank you for being a friend, an encourager, a pusher and a sister support.

Looking for Love in All the Wrong Places

Toni Riddick

Growing up I didn't have what most other children had, an active mother. As far back as I can remember my mother had a substance abuse issue that unfortunately consumed her life. She was not in a position where she could take care of her children. As a result of this, my younger brother, sister and I were raised by my grandmother. We knew my mother had an addiction issue but my grandmother did her very best to shield us from that part of my mother's life. My grandmother did all she could to make sure we had a normal life. Even though we were not privy to my mother's lifestyle the kids in the neighborhood were. Kids can be cruel at times and boy they were, at least the ones I grew up with. I was taunted and bullied about my mother's addiction all the time. It made me so sad for her.

My memory of my mother is very vague to be honest. I can only recall certain things that transpired during my childhood as they relate to my mother. I think I may have blocked a lot of it out. I can remember when she did come home (because she would be gone for days) she would be visibly abused. Black eyes, busted lips. I was so confused as to how another person could use their hands on another person like that. They had no regard for her or how her children would react seeing her that way. My brother and sister were much younger and didn't see some of the things I did.

Still to this day I do not know how she turned to that lifestyle. She had so much going for herself. She was a high school graduate and a college graduate. She started out great and I assume she ended up with the wrong crowd. My mother may have been looking for love in all the wrong places. As I began to truly realize my mother had a problem there was nothing I could do to help her as a child myself. Having to see her that way, she would come in high, drunk even sometimes, cursing at my grandmother because she wanted money and my granny refused.

I do remember her being admitted to the psychiatric hospital in Petersburg, VA. I was just a child going to visit my mother there. I was wondering why she was there. I did not know at the time she was having mental health issues as well. I didn't recognize her when we would visit. She would be so heavily medicated. I remember having an overwhelming sadness for her. My grandmother raised us in church so I knew what I could do to help my mother was to pray and talk to God. As an eight-year-old child I prayed for my mother. Having to see her in that condition it hurt my heart and I know it hurt my grandmother too. We never had a chance to talk about it either. I guess, like any black household, what goes on in the house stays in the house. I really wish it was not that way. I wish there was a way to have gotten her the real help she needed.

Sadly her lifestyle led to a life of destruction. When I was 11 years old some evil person decided they wanted to play God and take her life. She was murdered in August 1991 and dumped like garbage. Whomever committed this unspeakable act to my mother has never been caught now, 31 years later. They stabbed her over 16 times and just left her, dumped her body like she was trash. She was not trash. She was a mother of three children, a daughter, an aunt, a niece, a cousin. Her death left a void in our family. My grandmother took it very hard. My mother was her baby girl. My granny only had two girls.

It was hard growing up without my mom. Yes, I am so grateful for my grandmother, but she was older and didn't quite understand what I was going through sometimes. Being bullied a lot was very taxing on me as well. When people know your mother has an addiction or they see her out in the street high they want to joke about it. I did not think it was a joke.

I can say I did not have many friends growing up. I was a fighter. This is how I was able to cope with the constant bullying and teasing. "I am going to fight you."

I can remember being bullied and told by a great aunt, "You're going to be just like your momma."

That statement hurt me so much. I told my granny, "I never want to be around that lady ever again," and that was her sister. I have since forgiven her and moved on as I have kids growing up, but to hear that from a blood relation was terrible.

I vowed that day to break generational curses. Well, at least I tried to. Getting involved in dead-end relationships. Having children out of wedlock. I was seeking love. I never had a relationship with my father. I guess I was looking for that love in all those failed relationships I was in. Don't get me wrong; my grandmother loved us so very much. She took excellent care of us. However, I was seeking love from a father, a man. I never had it and I wanted that so badly. Someone to love me. Keep in mind I wanted to break generational curses. My mom had me at 16. I had my first daughter unmarried at age 21.

Running from relationship to relationship I was again looking for love. In all the wrong places. I knew my mother loved me, she just didn't show it much. She left us with my granny so I knew she loved us. We all go through struggles in life and this was just my mother's. While I was so angry that substance abuse controlled her life it didn't stop me from the path I chose to take in my late teens. Now listen, I was a force to be reckoned with and no one had a clue. Not sweet old church girl Toni, oh no.

I met a man still looking for love in the wrong places. He was, let's say, a big time drug dealer. He introduced me to the lifestyle of having anything I wanted and ever wished for, but it came at a cost. I have never done a drug in my life, never, but I sure could back then cook it, separate it, bag it, whatever needed to be done. This man who told me he loved me never really did. He just needed a dumb little girl to handle business for him. Looking back over that part of my life I just say wow. How could you ever do that knowing your mother had this very same issue? Here you are selling it to people, destroying families by giving these people this drug. I was never a street seller; I was in the "trap" (a home where drugs were prepared and sold). People coming in and out all hours of the day and night. Oh, by this time I had left my grandmother's house because her rules were too strict for me. I should have kept my little butt right there.

Can I just tell of the goodness of God right here? You may say, "How is God in this?" Well, the entire time I was at that "trap" it was never busted, robbed, shot up, nothing. Now, it did happen, but I was never around when it did.

God was looking out for me even when I wasn't looking out for myself. It began to get old so I just said, "Hey, I can't keep doing this." I could only think of my mother. *Do you realize the same drug your mother was addicted to you are destroying lives with?* Big reality check for me. Now listen, I was saved and had been. I just stopped going to church. Any church kid knows if you had to go all your life you can't wait until you're 18 to leave the coop. I wasn't living for God at all, but He still had His hand on my life. God will right your wrong!

As life continued to go on I was again in and out of relationships that meant me no good. Now, through all of this I was still saved, just not living according to the Word of God. One thing was for sure, God never took His hand off me. I guess that is the advantage of having a praying grandmother. I can remember her saying to me, "You may stray, but you won't stay." It meant you'll be back in church, in ministry, as I should have been wholeheartedly.

The prayers of my granny never went unanswered. God just had to wait for me to say yes. I love and appreciate my granny giving me Jesus. She introduced him to us at an early age. My granny wasn't the one who sent you to church, she was right there as well. I owe so much to her. She instilled in us the Word of the Lord. Sometimes we may steer away and go down the wrong road, but God is always there. Just in the nick of time! I can say I am proudly saved, sanctified and filled with the Holy Ghost. I serve the Lord with my whole heart and I try my best to instill in my children what my granny instilled in me. There is no place I would rather be than in the will of the Lord. It is safe and secure. I bless Him for keeping me even through my mess!

Do not think that you are too far gone that God can't come and sweep you right up! He can and He will. Submit to Him; live for Him. There is indeed a blessing in being on the Lord's side. I thank Him every day for His grace and mercy and His hand upon my life. I praise God for where I am now in ministry and where He is taking me. Keep the faith and never give up.

God will definitely right your wrong! Be encouraged!

Author Toni Riddick

Toni is a wife, mother, Elder, Evangelist, servant, daughter, sister and friend. Currently she is a member of Forever Fire Empowerment, LLC under the leadership of Prophetess Natasha Bibbins. She was baptized at the age of six. She was raised in church her entire life. God kept saying yes and she kept saying no—God Won! She was an MIT for about seven years before becoming a licensed and ordained minister/Evangelist in 2018. She holds an associate's degree in Social Sciences with a minor in Human Resource Management. Toni is currently pursuing her bachelor's degree in Theology from Holy Light Church of Deliverance Bible College, Bishop Samuel Carruth founder. Toni is married to Connie Riddick and the mother of five children, Dyamon, Ty'Kyiah, Tywan, Kadeiyn, and David. One of Toni's favorite pieces of scripture is II Cor 4:17-18 KJV – For our light affliction, which is but for a moment, worketh for us a far more exceeding and eternal weight of glory, while we look not at the things which are seen, but at the things which are not seen, for the things which are seen are temporal, but the things which are not seen are eternal.

Contact Information:

Facebook: Latoya Riddick
Email: jones.latoya4@yahoo.com

Toni's Acknowledgements

First, giving all honor to God. I thank Him for what He is doing in my life. I am excited for my future. I want to thank my grandmother, Deaconess Emmie L. White-Adams, for introducing me to Jesus. It is the best thing she ever did and taught me. I also want to thank my mentor, Prophetess Natasha, for her push. She pushes me in ways I never knew I could go. I am so thankful for my husband Connie Riddick and our children Dyamon, Ty'Kyiah, Tywan, Kadeiyn, and David. The Lord is truly amazing. If I had 10,000 tongues it would not be enough to thank Him.

Learning to Forgive

Melinda Peet

Synopsis

This chapter will take you through my journey that led me to make one the hardest decisions I ever had to make in my life, one that was unforgivable, or so I thought. I will take you through my process of how God rights my wrong and how it led to healing and forgiveness. Through our process, God will require something of us to receive healing, forgiveness, and freedom. It is our obedience to what God is telling us to do that leads us to that ultimate place. I pray that this chapter blesses you in a mighty way.

Is It Really Love?

I was a young woman in my twenties; I was at a happy time in my life. I was in a relationship with this kind and loving gentleman. He accepted and had developed a relationship with my three-year-old son I had from a previous relationship. He would pick my son up from daycare on days I was working late and take care of him until I got off, I really thought we were moving in a great direction. Our relationship was going well, I was in love, and I just knew that our next steps would lead to marriage.

One year, he got laid off from his job and the company I was working for was hiring so I told him to apply. My friends told me that might not be a clever idea, but I thought it would be great—we could ride to work together, we would be working in separate departments in different buildings, what could be so bad with that? He was hired with the company, we would ride in together, we would have lunch together and then drive home together after work. Everything was going well, and I was really enjoying the extra time we were having together.

As time went on, things began to change, and we started having some problems within our relationship. We would have many talks about how to make our relationship work; some discussions revolved around whether we wanted to stay together or go our separate ways, but through it all we were still spending a lot of time together. Eventually our work routine started to change. There would be some days when he told me he could not go to lunch because he had to work through his lunch; then some days we didn't drive in together because he had something to do after work. I never had a reason not to believe what he told me, so I never questioned it. Those "some days" turned into all the time, our work routine had come to a complete stop, but we were still seeing each other and spending time together outside of work.

A few months later, I received a promotion and had to move to a new department in the same building he worked in. With working in the same building, I thought this would be an opportunity for us to begin having lunch together again. We had lunch once or twice but never in the cafeteria. One day, I was walking past the cafeteria, which was all glass, headed to the restroom and I saw him having lunch with a young lady; he was smiling and talking and she was giggling. When I saw them, it took me back to the time we first met. I was the one sitting there giggling while he was smiling and talking, he was very charming. He never even saw me walk past. It took everything in me not to walk into that cafeteria and find out what was going on and let that young lady know I was his girl. I had to keep my cool and not make a scene at work, so I waited until we were together that evening.

I told him that I saw him having lunch with this young lady and asked what was going on. He told me they were just friends, and I took him at his word. You know how we do, when we have that gut feeling that it is a lie, but we love him, so we believe what he says. So, I pushed past what I was feeling, and we continued in this so-called relationship.

As the weeks went on, I would see him go by her desk and they would chit chat, I would see them talking in the cafeteria all while my time with him at work got less and less. I could hear what my friends said to me playing in my head, "I do not think it is a clever idea for you both to work together." I never thought I had anything to worry about and he would tell me the same thing.

Of course, we all know what happens when you are spending a lot of time with one person and what that can lead to. It eventually went from talking at work to spending time outside of work. One night he left my house, he was in a bit of a hurry and left something behind. I tried to catch him before he pulled off, but he was already gone. I got in my car to take it to him because, to honest, something did not feel right about how quickly he left—woman's intuition?

As I was approaching his house, I saw this same young lady from work get out of her car and they went into the house together. My heart dropped to my feet and anger began to boil up inside of me. I got out my car to ring the doorbell and as I approached the door, I could see his mother through the window. My heart shattered just at the thought of her knowing about this woman. All kinds of thoughts were going through my head; I wanted to bust the door down but did not want to disrespect his mother. These thoughts ran through my head all night so I could not sleep. I would call his phone and not get an answer. Seeing them together at work just kept playing in my head and the more I thought about it the more I realized that she must not know about me. We were all in the same building;

you could see straight through the different departments. I had walked past her, but she never even looked at me in a way that would make me think she knew that he and I were together.

The next day, when I arrived at work, I decided to approach her and give her the real story. I introduced myself and I told her that he and I were in a relationship, we had experienced a few problems that we were trying to work through. She told me he had never told her about me and that she wished I would have come to her earlier because she had started having feelings for him. I could not believe what she had just said to me; so, in other words, she was telling me she was not going to stop seeing him. When I approached him regarding what I saw the night before and the conversation with her, he still tried to say nothing was going on and that they were just friends.

He told me he would come by that night so that we could talk. Later that day, I saw the two of them talking. I am not sure what he said to her, but it was evident she did not believe it by what happened next. That night, he came by my house so that we could talk and while we were talking my doorbell rang, and it was her. She stated that she was at his house, and he was rushing to leave, and something did not feel right so she followed him. Hmmm, does that sound familiar?

I told her that he was there and to let me go get him. He must have heard her voice while we were talking because when I went to get him, he was no longer in my room. I looked all over the house and could not find him. I saw that my back door was cracked, and it was not previously open. I went out the back door and saw him hiding behind a tree. Yes, hiding like a coward. I told him his new girl was at the front door, that he was a liar and a coward, and this so-called relationship we had was over. I locked my back door; then I walked back to the front door and told her he was hiding in the backyard if she wanted him.

I told her she could have him; I did not have time for the lies and games, and I shut the door. I was so heartbroken and disappointed in myself for letting myself get caught up in this mess. I dreaded going to work every day because I knew I would have to see them, and it was apparent they were still involved. So, I decided to resign from my job because that was something I could no longer look at every day and I completely left him alone.

What Is a Girl to Do?

A month after we had parted ways, I realized that I did not get my monthly cycle. At first, I thought it was from all the stress of what I had just been through. A week or two later, I still did not have my cycle and at that point I became worried. So, I decided to take a pregnancy test. At first glance I thought my eyes were deceiving me. I shook the test strip and looked again, and it was positive. I could not believe what was happening to me, I was trying to heal from this heartbreak only to find out that I was pregnant by my ex, the very person who just broke my heart.

I struggled with calling him to let him know, I did not even want to talk to him after what he had done to me. I finally picked up the phone and called and asked him to come by so we could talk. We sat down and I told him I had missed my cycle and decided to take a test and the test had come back positive. I pulled out the test to show him and told him that I wanted to have an abortion. He was totally against it and wanted me to have the baby, he stated he would be in our baby's life and take care of our child. Thoughts began to run through my head; maybe this would be what would bring us back together. And then he said, "But we will not be together."

I felt like I was being stabbed in my heart all over again, all I could do was cry and I became so angry. I told him if we would not be together, then I did not want to carry his child. He asked me not to abort our child, to take a few days and think about it. Those next few days I could barely sleep or eat. I struggled with the thought of having yet another child and not being with the father and providing the family that I wanted my children to have. I called him and told him I could not have this baby and I wanted him to help me pay for this abortion. He refused to help me in any way and continued to try to talk me into having the baby. I refused and the next day I called and scheduled an appointment at the abortion clinic.

That week I waited for my appointment was torture for me; I was so hurt and I could not believe the direction my life was going in. He kept calling and leaving messages, trying to convince me to change my mind, but I would not take his calls.

The day of the abortion my best friend took me to the clinic and as we sat there, she asked me, "Are you sure you want to do this?

And I told her, "Yes. There is no way I am having another child out of wedlock."

The nurse called my name and took me into the back; she gave me a gown to put on and told me the doctor would be arriving in a few minutes to do an ultrasound before the procedure. Those few minutes were the longest minutes of my life.

The doctor came in; I laid down on the table and he proceeded to do the ultrasound. A minute later the doctor said, "Oh, my goodness."

I began to worry and asked the doctor if something was wrong. He turned the monitor around and said to me, "This is not something that usually shows up so early in pregnancy on an ultrasound. You are carrying twins."

As I looked at the monitor tears just began to fall down my face and I began to cry so hard that I could barely catch my breath. The doctor printed the ultrasound picture of my twins, handed it to me and told me he would give me a few minutes to decide whether I wanted to move forward or not.

I got up, put on my clothes, and went back to the lobby. As I sat there crying and telling my best friend what had happened, she just tried to console me and told me she would be there for me whatever I decided to do. I picked up the phone and I called my ex to tell him that I was at the clinic to have the abortion and during the ultrasound the doctor had told me I was carrying twins. He began to cry and begged me not to abort our children. He said to me again, "I will be there for you and the kids, but we will not be together."

 I hung up the phone and my thoughts began to race in my head; I felt like my head was going to explode. *What did I do so wrong? What is wrong with me that this man wants these babies and not me?* I sat there so hurt and so angry, telling myself there was no way I could take care of twins and my son on my own. How could I have two more babies out of wedlock?

I wanted my children to have their mother and father together. I knew what it felt like not to have that and I did not want that for my children. Yes, my son's father was in his life, he took care of him and spent time with him, but I wanted more for him and the twins I was carrying, but I knew it would not happen. I called him back and I said, "I cannot do it."

He cried as he kept saying, "Do not do this."

I replied, "I cannot keep these babies." I said goodbye and hung up the phone.

I got up and walked to the reception counter and told them to tell the doctor I was ready to proceed with the abortion. I held that ultrasound picture so tight in my hand and cried as I walked to the back. I put it in my pocket as I began to get undressed for the procedure. I put on the gown, laid on the table and cried until I was put to sleep. I went through the procedure and as I woke up, I was still crying.

As I was getting dressed, I checked my pocket to make sure the ultrasound picture of my babies was still there. I cried all the way home and from that day forward I never spoke to my ex again. I got home and I put my picture in my keepsake box and told myself I must move forward, heal, and get my life together for me and my son. When I put my ultrasound picture of my babies in that keepsake box, I never talked about it again. I pushed it so deep down on the inside of me so that I would never have to think about what I did so that I could move on with my life.

The Healing Process

A few years had gone by, and I met someone. After dating for a year, he secretly asked my parents for my hand in marriage and surprised me with his proposal. I said yes, and a year after the proposal we got married. As all married couples do, we discussed having children. He was okay with not having any, even though he had no children. I felt relief because I did not want any more children because of the trauma I went through in my decision to abort my twins, but a part of me felt like I needed to give my husband a child of his own. He assured me it was okay, but little did we know there was already a bun in the oven. The first year of our marriage I gave birth to our son and four years later I gave birth to our daughter. We were happy; we had our three children; we bought a home; I became a stay-at-home mom and life was good.

Before I knew it, fifteen years had gone by and what I never thought would happen did happen. My marriage ended in divorce. I began to pick up the pieces of my heart yet again, and as time went on, I began to date my current husband and we began going to church together. I was excited about this because I had not been to church in some years, but I was praying and spending time with God daily. I began desiring a deeper more intimate relationship with God, but I felt like there was a hindrance; I began praying and asking God to show me what was hindering me from growing a deeper relationship with Him. I have always been a dreamer and God has always spoken to me in dreams.

One night, while I was sleeping, I had a dream that I was being dragged around a room by a spirit. I was fighting trying to get loose, but I couldn't break loose. While I was being dragged around the room, the things I had done in my life were played out before my eyes. When I got to the end of the room the spirit released me and said, "Remember that abortion?" I jumped out of my sleep and began crying, repenting, and asking God to forgive me for having that abortion. The next morning, I woke up and as I went into the bathroom to get ready for church, I just began to cry out to God for forgiveness and while I was crying out, I heard the Holy Spirit say, "Share it."

I began to tell God, "I am not sharing my business in front of people at church."

And again, I heard, "Share it."

I told God I could not do that and again He said, "Share it."

Then the Holy Spirit said, "Obedience is better than sacrifice."

I came out of the bathroom and began to tell my husband about the dream and what I heard the Holy Spirit speak to me. I wrestled with it all the way to church and in my head

I was telling myself, *I'm not going to do it.* When we arrived at church, our Pastor's Bishop got up to speak a few words and when he said the word "obedience" I began to rock back and forth in my chair, and I could not sit still. God was dealing with me so strongly that I could not refuse to do what He had told me to do. I tapped my husband and told him to tell our pastor I had something to share. When I heard that word "obedience," it struck me like lightning; it was no coincidence that my pastor was also just teaching about obedience in bible study that week.

I took the microphone, and I began to share my dream. When I got to the part where the spirit released me and said, "Remember that abortion," three women in the church began to cry out. I began to share how I had to repent for my sin because it had been holding me in bondage all these years. That day not only were the shackles broken off those two women, but out of my obedience and repentance the shackles were broken off me and I felt a release. I went home that afternoon thanking and praising God for what He had done. I was so glad I was obedient, but God was not finished with me.

That night, during my prayer time, the Holy Spirit spoke again and told me to call my ex to repent and ask for his forgiveness for aborting our twins and that I needed to forgive myself. I told God, "I did what you told me to do this morning, I have not talked to my ex in twenty years, he will not want to talk to me and how do I know his number is still the same?"

Again, I heard, "Obedience is better than sacrifice," and the Holy Spirit reminded me of what I asked God. *What is hindering me from growing into a deeper relationship with you?*

So, I prayed, and I asked God to touch his heart to receive what I had to say. I picked up the phone and called; I couldn't believe the number was the same. I apologized to him for not taking into consideration his feelings and reacting drastically out of my emotions. I repented and asked if he could forgive me for not have given him a chance to be the father he wanted to be to our twins, and he said yes. Tears began to fall down my face and I thanked him and wished him well. After our conversation, I took that ultrasound picture; as I held it in my hands with tears still running down my face, I asked my babies to forgive me for not giving them the chance at life and at that point I felt total peace, and I was able to truly release everything and forgive myself.

Finally Seeing the Light

Looking back over my journey, I did not realize back then, when my twins showed up on that ultrasound picture, something the doctor stated never happened at that stage of pregnancy, that God was trying give me a sign not to make the decision I was about to make. I was so blinded by my emotions, the anger and all the pain, that I ignored it and selfishly aborted my babies. I never took my ex's feelings into consideration; I just did not want any part of him. I wanted him to feel the pain I was feeling from our breakup, and I allowed that to cause me to make a terrible decision that kept me bound for 20 years and in a place that hindered me from growing in a deeper relationship with God.

I had thought I was healed, I thought I had moved passed it, but I just pushed it so deep down into a dark place that I could not see it or deal with it. Until that day I prayed that prayer asking God to show me what was hindering me from growing a deeper relationship with Him. God answered that prayer by showing me through my dream and shining His light on that deep, dark area and digging up the very hindrance that was the sin of abortion, bitterness, anger, and unforgiveness. It was through my obedience in repenting and asking forgiveness not only from God but my ex and me, along with God's love, grace, and mercy for me, that I was forgiven by God, my ex and myself. It was at that moment that God truly healed my heart, and I no longer had this false sense of healing.

I am forever grateful to God for righting my wrong by bringing me to repentance and having me share my testimony, so that other women who have gone through the same experience can be healed and set free, and blessing me with two more children. If there is one thing I can say to help and encourage you it is this. Whatever pain or trauma you have gone through or are going through, whether it is self-inflicted or caused by someone else, you need to truly take the time to heal the right way, God's way. Not by pushing your feelings, emotions, and pain so deep down that you can't face or deal with them. We need to turn inward and face what we have gone through and forgive ourselves and those who may have hurt us; that is the only way true healing can take place and we can truly be set free. Remember obedience is better than sacrifice!

Author Melinda Peet

As a devout follower of Christ, Melinda Peet—a mother, wife, and entrepreneur—uplifts and empowers believers with the tools essential to cultivating an intimate relationship with God through her vision "The Get Up Movement". Over the five months Melinda recovered in her home following an unfortunate car accident, she began to draw closer to God in a way that was recognizably different than any previous time. She began to hear the Lord speak, repeatedly telling her to "GET UP". Confused at first, Melinda prayed for understanding. The Lord began to reveal that He wanted her to "Get Up" from those things in her past that had kept her bound in life. These things blocked her from having a closer relationship with God, thereby delaying her from stepping into her purpose. Deep-rooted fears and unrepented sins going back years were brought to light and "getting up" from these things that held her down allowed God to graciously work within her. In the midst of this He blessed her with the inspiration for The Get Up Movement.

The Get Up Movement's mission is to assist and encourage believers to do exactly what the Lord placed in Melinda's heart to do: To get up from that dark place, get up from those things keeping us from moving forward in our relationship with the Lord. To get up from the obstacles restraining us from advancing in our God-given visions and His unique plans for us all! From a young girl and to this very day she has always been deeply compassionate, displaying empathy for those who may feel lost, are hurting or in need of encouragement. Melinda has a servant's heart and the spirit of a prayer warrior and will stand in the gap and in agreement with you in prayer. Take part in the movement by tuning in to the Get Up Movement's Facebook Live with Melinda and guests. Before you can change your life, you have to believe change is possible. Join the movement today! "When God says move, Get Up from what has you bound," - Melinda Peet.

Contact Information:

Facebook: Melinda Peet
Facebook: The Get Up Movement
Clubhouse: Melinda Peet
Instagram: Melinda Peet
Email: melindapeet1@gmail.com

For His Glory

Ayanna Lynnay

Synopsis

Nazareth! Can anything good come from there? Nathanael asked.... I love this interaction that takes place when Philip is attempting to tell Nathanael that they had found Jesus, the One whom Moses wrote about and the One the prophets had spoken about. But instead of being excited the first thing Nathanael asked is how could anything good come from that place... Sadly this is the same commentary that many people still face when they have a past. Can anything good come from a person who was a troubled runaway teen who was labeled emotionally disturbed by the school system? I present....

I am one of those people who feels nothing in life came easy for me. When I look back at where I have been and where I am, it seems that everything I achieved or obtained was a result of a fight. Me fighting against me and many of the bad decisions that I made (and still sometimes make). What I did not realize for the first 27 years of my life was that this fight is fixed and I was predestined to be who God has called me to be. The journey to becoming that woman, well, it has been and continues to be just that, a journey.

Many people have hard lives because of the treatment and decisions of other people. Children suffer daily due to people who have the capability to become a parent but never should be a parent. That isn't my testimony. Although my father was a drug addict who allowed his addiction to uproot him from our home and his responsibilities, I had (and thank God still have) a wonderful strong mother who understood the power of prayer. Life was not easy when the former breadwinner shrugged off all responsibilities and left the mother with two young children (my older sister was married and out of the house) to shoulder all the responsibilities that unexpectedly were dropped into her lap. My little sister Melody was about nine months old and my mom was only working part-time, certainly not enough to provide for all that she needed to take care of; but, as I mentioned, she prayed and somehow, some way, the Lord always made a way.

I mention my childhood because I believe that was the catalyst for a lot of bad decisions I made later in life. My father and I were close, so to see him leave the house and vow never to take care of us just to hurt my mother caused deep emotional damage that I did not realize until years and years later. My teenage years were exceptionally bad. I stayed in trouble at school to the point where I eventually had to go to a special school for children with behavioral problems that could not be managed in public school. I put my poor mother through the ringer as she was trying her best to take care of us and I made her job 1000x harder. I had no interest in doing the right things like going to school and trying to learn. Nope, instead I skipped school, got into fights, drank alcohol, smoked weed and dated much older guys.

Although my mother was a woman of prayer we did not regularly go to church due to my mother's work schedule and even when we did I never paid any attention to what was being said. I had no interest in anything other than what I wanted to do. I knew nothing about having a personal relationship with the Lord. I don't remember the churches we went to having an active youth department or really ministering to those who were my age. I just remember going to church, being bored and not understanding what they were talking about. Another memory is going to church with one of my girlfriends whose father was a pastor and being in church all day. I was still bored, still did not understand what they were talking about and now I was hungry. I remember thinking I would never go back to one of those holiness/Pentecostal type churches again.

As I reflect back on my younger ages there was absolutely nothing that showed any inclination that I would be anything other than a troubled teen and a statistic. I had no hopes or dreams (other than wanting to be rich, lol). My attitude was so bad that even if someone did come to me to try to give me some words of advice it would have gone in one ear and right out the other. My mother tried to do whatever she could. She tried placing me in a Christian school, which had little impact, or so I thought. I remember there was some kind of service we had and a teacher prayed for me. I remember feeling a feeling I had never felt before and I wanted more. I did not know what it was at the time, but I felt the presence of God and gave my heart to the Lord. I think I even started speaking in tongues. Unfortunately, that early fire was soon quenched as I had no one to help fuel it. Little did I know none shall be plucked out of the Lord's hand. I believe with everything in me because I gave my life to the Lord and because of the prayers of my grandmother, mother and whoever else prayed for me, my life was sealed. No weapon that was formed against me was able to prosper against me.

There were many weapons formed against me. Sadly many of those weapons were able to form due to some of the poor decisions I made. Why would I make the decision to run away from home and go halfway around the country at the age of 17? Why would I decide to get involved with drugs after seeing how they destroyed my father's life? Why didn't I care about school and almost dropped out in the 12th grade? Why did I involve myself with people who could not have cared less about me? I will tell you why—because I did not know who I was, whose I was and what I was called to do. I simply lived life under a dark cloud. Wanting and desiring more but not know what that more was.

It was because I did not know who I was, whose I was or what my purpose was that the enemy tried to destroy me. I was so busy trying to run and seek after those people and things that would give me good feelings and distract me from my mundane life that I did not realize that I was on a slippery slope going down fast.

BUT GOD! There are three life-changing experiences I will not forget. The first was going to a friend of mine's memorial service. Even how I found out about it was divine. One day, I was looking through the paper at the obituary section and I saw a small announcement that said someone I once had a crush on growing up had drowned saving his children. The announcement stated his memorial service was going to be held a few days later. I called my girlfriend Leah who also knew him and we made plans to go. When we got there, it was a pretty uneventful service. At the end everyone was going up to hug his mother. Right before I got to his mother the pastor of the church jumped in between me and his mother and said over me, "Devil, you can't have her." I was mortified! Was she talking to me?

I looked up. The pastor seemingly stared into my soul and said, "The devil wants to destroy you, but he can't have you."

She then instructed me to call on the name of Jesus, which I did in a sort of whisper, and she made me keep saying, "Jesus," louder and louder. I remember wanting to get out of that place. I was like, *I did not come to a memorial service for all of this.* When I finally got out of there, I told my girlfriend that woman was crazy, but deep down I knew that she wasn't.

The second life-changing experience came in the summer of 1993. I had just returned home after running away and being gone for three months. I was lying in my mother's bed and I glanced over and saw her Bible. I picked it up for some reason and out fell a letter. My mother had written a letter to the Lord asking for Him to bring me home safely and was begging for Him to save my life. To save me from me and all of the poor decisions I had been making. I was 17 at the time and I remember crying because I was causing so much pain to my mom. I wanted to change but I did not know how. I remember wondering, *What is wrong with me? Why do I keep doing the things I do?*

A few months later, I got pregnant with my daughter Shakiya. For most people being pregnant at 17 and having a baby at 18 would have been terrible, but for me it actually was a life-saver. I was so miserable being back home. My mother and I constantly fought and I was planning on running away again. Right as I packed up and was preparing to leave I found out I was pregnant. This obviously caused me to rethink some things. Because I was pregnant and was always in trouble in school I was allowed to be home schooled. My guidance counselor Ms. Torres offered to be my instructor and I was able to graduate from high school on time with the rest of my class without missing a beat. I was six months pregnant. Although I often got in trouble in school I was smart. When my daughter was one year old, I was able to go to nursing school and a year later I became a licensed practical nurse. I eventually went on to become a registered nurse with a master's degree. The one who no one thought would ever amount to anything…. BUT GOD….

The third life-changing experience came in April 2003. I was at friend's house; we had been partying and drinking. All of a sudden, she said, "I am going to put on a church tape."

I told her, "I don't want to watch no church service." But she was insistent.

As she was going to put the VHS in to play her foot got caught on something on the floor. As she started to bleed she said, "See, the devil don't want me to play the tape, but I am playing it anyway." She hopped over to the VHS player and put the tape in. My life was forever changed.

The message was preached by Evangelist Rita Twiggs at T.D. Jakes' Woman Thou Art Loose Conference. To be honest I do not remember one word that was preached, but it hit my spirit. It was like a bright light had just been turned on after 27 years of me being in darkness. SUDDENLY things that had happened in my life began to make sense. This was the beginning of me starting to learn who I was, whose I was, and the first inclination that God had a divine purpose and a plan for my life.

Obviously there is so much more, but since this is just a chapter and not a whole book I have to stop. My purpose in sharing this is to encourage that mother, that father, grandparent or family member who is praying for that troubled youth or any other family member who looks like they will never amount to anything. I want you to know I am a testament to the power of prayer. My family was praying for me when I was hopelessly lost. At the appointed time God answered those prayers in the most unusual way. While I was high and drunk. He brought me out of darkness into His marvelous light.

I also want to encourage that person who is out there and seems like they made such a mess of their life and there is no way God can use them. I made so many bad decisions and choices before AND after I gave my life to Christ that I am deeply humbled and thankful for any time the Lord uses me to be a blessing to someone else in any capacity. It puts me in mind of the scripture Luke 7:47 (NIV): *Therefore, I tell you, her many sins have been forgiven—as her great love has shown.* See when God has forgiven you for so much, you have the tendency to love much. God is looking to use people who love Him and love His people. Your old mess becomes a message of love and hope for someone else! As you stand up full of God's love, being used to help someone else, you too will look back over all your *wrongs* and see how the Lord has made them *right* for His Glory.

Author Ayanna Lynnay

Ayanna is an author and founder of ChosenButterfly Publishing where books that transform lives are published. She has co-written many books dealing with the subjects of women in ministry, divorce, finding your purpose, living your dreams and more. Her first solo book project, titled *Devil, Please, I Am Not Offended,* deals with the relationship-destroying spirit of offense. ChosenButterfly Publishing has published over 40 books, some of which were Amazon #1 bestsellers in their category.

Ayanna wears many titles—wife, mother, minister, nurse, author, book publisher, mentor, etc.—but the title she takes most joy in is the title of transformed servant of the Lord. Sharing the message of hope and the power of God's transformation is the hallmark of how the Lord uses her. If you have ever heard her minister you will agree that she is real, relatable, transparent, easy to understand, powerful and yet humble. With a life dedicated to the Lord, Ayanna is transforming into the woman she never knew she could be and helping to transform other lives as well.

You can contact her via Facebook: https://www.facebook.com/AyannaLynnay

Have book in you that you been itching to get out? Let 's Go! www.cb-publishing.com

God's Love Is Amazing

—————— ⟨⟩ ——————

Dr. Natasha Bibbins

Synopsis:

Life has a way to throw curves in your life that will make you doubt God. When you want to do good things, evil things from your past creep up to remind you that you are not worthy of God's unfailing love. At some point in your life's story, you must see that every failure is followed by a victory. Just think about that for a moment. You may have lost a job, but you got another one. No matter what it was that made you feel like you were not loved, take another look because God has taken your WRONGS and made them RIGHT!

Is my future over because of my past?

The Eastern Shore of Virginia was a place where not many people chose to dream big. Dreams and aspirations were only for those people who were considered to be on the higher end of the scope. Those people would include the judge, the police officers, the lawyers, the doctors, and maybe the nurses; but not many people in my range were expected to make good choices. As a result of that, I made many mistakes; some, I must admit, I thought were funny, but through it all, God has truly righted my wrongs.

The purpose of this book is to share some of the testimonies and truths of people just like you, to let you know that no matter what decisions you have made, God is still there. In my darkest moments, God was there. When I thought life was over, God was there. When I made my bed in hell, God was there. When I messed up … yes, God was there! In July 2020, God gave me the vision to share my testimony and to invite others to share their testimonies on how God will turn your story around for your good. You see, I have not always lived a life of sanctification; to tell the truth, I loved the world more than I loved God. But when God has a plan for your life, it really does not matter what road you take because He will download His GPS in you to get you back on the right path to righteousness.

How can a person who loved the world and the things of the world more than God be used by God? How could

He trust me with riches and abundance, when I love them more than I love Him? The Bible says, "*For the love of money is the root of all evil: which while some coveted after, they have erred from the faith, and pierced themselves through with many sorrows*" (1 Timothy 6:10). Timothy already identified that the love of money is the root of evil; however, I loved money and nice things. I grew up on welfare and working on the farms in the morning before school and after school; I promised myself that I would never live that way again. The realization is that I felt that money and the things of this world could do for me more than God could never do. I was wrong.

Growing up in church, I saw and heard things that made me doubt if God was real. There were many nights that I cried myself to sleep wondering if God could hear my cry. Just imagine being told that you are going to hell just for waking up in the morning. Really it was no reason to go to church if no matter what you did, you were still going to hell. So instead of searching for God, I searched for other things that would bring me joy, or what I considered to be joy. I wish I could tell you that I only searched out the things of God, but that would be a lie. You see, I was blessed with a talent that would allow me to generate the money I needed to take care of my children and myself, I did not need God's help. Well, at least that is what I thought. I had money but I still cried myself to sleep at night. I had money but still struggled to have friends who truly loved me. I had money but did not have a husband. I had money, but I was missing JOY! I had not one but two babies by the same man but without being married or committed. I felt embarrassed because other co-workers would talk about their husbands and their children, and all I could talk about were my children. How could I allow myself to fall into a trap like that? It was simple, I was looking for that joy. If no one else loved me, I knew that my babies did.

Can I assure you, yes you, that no matter what you have gone through in your past life, it has nothing to do with your future? Jeremiah 29:11 states, *"For I know the thoughts that I think toward you, saith the Lord, thought of peace, and of evil, to give you an expected end,"* so no matter how you started, or if the twists and turns of life have gotten you down, God still has the final say.

God will right any wrong that you may have done if you only believe and only believe that He can and will do just what He says. As I journey down my life, I pray that my experiences will allow you to see that no matter what you see today, it has nothing to do with the person I was. Me sharing my story is only to inspire you to dream big, push forward, to not allow your past to dictate your future.

As you read this book, I pray that it sparked a light that will allow you to forgive yourself and move forward toward the things that God has prepared for your future. We have all made mistakes, and we have all fallen short of the glory of

God, but because of grace and mercy, we can be who we are today. Do not discount who you are because of past failures. Embrace who you are today and just give God glory. For God is working this thing out just for you and when you come out you will not even have the residue from some of the things that you had to deal with in your past. Again, God will RIGHT your WRONG!

I Did Not Like the Person Inside of Me!

I did not like the person who was living inside of me. This person was sad, did not feel loved, and was not happy with the way she looked. I always wanted to be someone else. I would dream of being a movie star or someone everybody would gravitate toward. That was not the case for me. Being someone who is made fun of, talked about, and often mistreated can drive a person to do some things that would be considered wrong. When you hate yourself, you tend to want to fit in with others, just to be accepted.

I know a lot of us do not like to speak on this topic, but, to be free, it's a MUST. Not feeling as if you are loved by your family as a child can really have issues that follow you to your future, if you are not delivered. No, I was not delivered; I was not set free of my past. I even hated to look at myself in the mirror because I did not like what I saw. I did not have anyone to remind me that I was "fearfully and wonderfully made." I could not understand why I had to be born with "green eyes". Again, there was no one there to say to me that "God designed you just the way He wanted you." I searched but there was nobody who could lift me up for being different; instead, I continued to hate my eyes! Before we go any further, let me remind you that you are fearfully and wonderfully made by God. God designed you just the way He wanted you. He needs for you to be unique so that when He looks in a crowd of people, he can see His baby standing there from afar.

As I grew older, I was still unhappy because I was tall, skinny, and with burnt-red hair. I wished I was shorter, I wished I was fat, and I wanted black hair. I guess you could say I was not satisfied with the person I was. If you do not begin to love the person God designed you to be, you will never find happiness. If you never find happiness within yourself, you will continue to make wrong decisions and wrong choices. Yes, I made some bad decisions and bad choices that could have cost me my freedom, BUT GOD. God will take a bad situation and turn it into a great situation.

Why is it important to love yourself? That's simple, Mark 12:31 is one of God's greatest commandments and that is to "Love your neighbor as yourself." It is impossible to love your neighbor without loving yourself first. This is a commandment from the Lord. If this is what the Lord requires, then why is it so difficult? As we journey through life we make a lot of mistakes but never realize that it's because we really do not like the person inside of us. I remember getting directions to look at the same mirror that I would look at every day and say, "I AM ENOUGH!" Well, I do not feel like I am enough, so why would I say it when I am trying to love the person inside of me?

My prayer is that we all would come to the realization of God's hand on and life and see that His thoughts for us are higher than our thoughts, that you may change your mind on how you see yourself when you look at yourself in the mirror. Allow that beautiful person from the inside to shine through to the outside, that you may be an encourager just by your walk. Love who you are.

Is My Childhood to Blame?

Most people often refer to the way they were raised as the reason why they make bad decisions or bad choices. You would hear a quote like, "I always did it like this," or "That is how my momma used to do it." Some fortunate people who were raised with their fathers in the home would say, "This is how my father taught me to do this." No matter what your reason for doing what you are doing or did in the past, it's because we make choices according to learned behavior.

Being a country girl born and raised on the Eastern Shore of Virginia I wish I could say that country living was great for me, but it was not. As young girls, working seems to be what we did best. We had to get up early in the morning before school to go and work in a field or on a farm and then go to school only to come back home from school and go back into the field again. This caused me to have a lot of pain and a lot of hatred. Yes, you can say that this book will give you a deeper view of who Natasha Walker really is. I had a lot of hatred inside of me because of my past. Being raised where you did what your mother told you to do, and that was the end of the story. There were times when I needed answers but was not allowed to ask a question. I would always say as a young girl that my children would never experience life the way I had to experience life; not to say that it was all bad, but at least 75% of it was. All I wanted was to be loved by my family. I tried to find love in the home, in the schools, in the neighborhoods, and with my friends. This was not always the case.

The Bible talks about love and how we should love one another with all of our hearts, but what if your heart is tainted? How do you love when there has never been a great example of love around you? I could not find love in the places where I was looking. I began to look for love in all the wrong places and found it. I was able to find love in drinking alcohol; I was able to find love in going to the clubs; I was even able to find love, well, at least what I thought was love, in men. When the first man said, "I love you," I fell for it. I was abused, cheated on, and even had one threaten me with a gun, but I still thought it was love. I would blame myself for the things I was going through, not realizing that I was not to blame. I have asked myself, *Was it my childhood that kept me believing that the abuse was my fault?* I often wondered if I had felt loved as a child, or if I felt like I was pretty as a child, or if I felt like people thought I was special, would I have settled for all the abuse?

If you are reading this right now and it is starting to make you feel or think about your childhood, I pray that God will deliver you from your past. I pray that when you take another look in the mirror you will see a beautiful person from the inside out. Decree and declare over your life that your past will no longer affect your future because we release it into the atmosphere so that you will never struggle because of your childhood again. Just because your grandmother did it, your mother did it, or your father did it does not mean you are going to do it. The curse has been broken, in the name of Jesus.

Releasing that prayer into the atmosphere shows that you are ready to be free. Freedom will remind you that you are special in God's sight. No longer will you use the excuse that you are the way you are because of your past. There is a song that says, "You love me through my good, you love me through my bad, you did not erase my future just because of my past, I am so glad that you loved me through my good and my bad." God's love is so amazing because His love covers a multitude of sins, 1 Peter 4:8. With this in mind, you can be sure to know that no matter what you have done in the past, God has already covered up your sins. Do not allow the mistakes of your past to define your future. Know that God is still changing your story as He rights your wrong. Keep living and keep striving.

Searching For Love!

Under the bed, in the closet, under the couch, in money, in cars, or in houses, still couldn't find love. Searching for love in all the wrong places can lead you to a dark and frustrating place. I was searching for someone to love me. I searched high and low but still could not find the love I was looking for. I did not realize that the love I was missing was only going to come from the Lord. The problem is I did not want the love from the Lord, I wanted it from a man or people. I can admit that I would get upset to see people loving on one another, I would even find myself getting jealous of other mother-and-daughter relationships. All I wanted was to feel the highest form of love. That love that I read about but never felt. That "Agape Love!" Yes, you know, that great example of love that was shown in John 15:13: "*Greater love has no one than this, that someone lay down his life for his friends.*" Yes, that is love. I want that love. I searched but still could not find that love.

One of the things I did not recognize until I searched for love within myself was that I did not love myself. How can one love themselves when they really do not know what love is? I wanted to love me but found it easier to love "them". I even settled for abuse just to be loved. The truth is I really didn't know that I was being abused because all I knew was abuse. I had searched all over but really could not find anybody who would love me unconditionally and would give me that agape love that my heart so desired. It was almost like I had gone searching for something that clearly was not there. We say searching for love in all the wrong places, but what if love is in front of you but you do not recognize that is love? I really thank God for never leaving me even when I was in those wrong places. I tried to drink love in me, and I tried to be with different men to have love on me. I even tried to smoke marijuana to feel love around me, but none of it worked. The truth is that was not the plan that God had for my life.

See the truth is we do not recognize when love is right in front of us. God was right there all the time. He promised in His Word that He would never leave me, nor would He forsake me; so even in those dark times of my life, God was still there. Even when I tried alcohol God was still there. As a reminder for you, God is still in your situation. He is still there and He is holding out His righteous right hand, waiting on you to just reach out and touch Him. Once you have truly been touched by God, you will never be the same.

As a young girl, I loved to sing and one of my many favorite artists was Stephanie Mills. She sang a song that said, "I

NEVER knew love like this before," and once I experienced God, I began to sing that song, but it was different. I was not singing it to a man; I started singing it to God. I said to God, "I never knew love like this before and once I was lost and now I am found and, God, you have turned my world around since I let you into my life." God's love for me is unexplainable and undeniable. No longer do I look for love because I am love! I have been rebuilt on love. This person who did not like to see others happy is the same person who encourages and prays for everyone to find happiness within them through God. Once again, God had to change me so that I could feel what love is. God continues to change my wrongs and make them all right.

Love Found Me!

So many of us struggle with this same thing where we are not ready to accept the obvious, which is that we really need to love ourselves before we can love another. After the Lord had me in isolation, I found myself and started loving myself. During this period of loving myself, I was able to see who God was through me. I always loved to pray, but love made my prayers come alive. If Jesus is love, and we say that Jesus lives in us, we are lying if we are not loving ourselves first. The Bible says in 1 Corinthians 16:14, "*Let all your things be done with charity,*" in other words, let everything be done in love. Jesus was the love that found me. Through all the mistakes I have made, God found me.

When I wanted to commit suicide, Jesus said, "No," and love found me. The moment when I discounted myself, Jesus found me.

The day I said, "I do not deserve to be happy," Jesus found me and brought me JOY! I wondered, *how can a person like me, one who made so many mistakes, be loved by God?* Although I never persecuted the church, my heart was not in the right place. Matthew 22:37 says, "*Jesus said unto him, Thou shalt love the Lord thy God with all thy heart, and with all thy soul, and all thy mind.*"

My heart was far from God. I even went as far as to say, "I do not need God," because I had money.

Can God really anoint someone who has been so full of mess? The answer is yes. God will clean you up by making your wrongs right and anoint you for your assignment. You will move from the back to the front because He will make you whole again. It is so amazing to know that God will still favor you after you have been less than perfect. God will still protect you when you find yourself in spaces and places that are not a part of your purpose.

I remember when I was in the nightclub one Thursday night; I know it was a Thursday because it was a Thanksgiving night. Having a feeling that something was going to happen, we stayed in the nightclub. As the night continued, a fight broke out right in front of me. So what it was a fight? Well, that small fight soon went from a small fight to a big gun fight. Afraid out of my mind, I wanted to leave, but my keys were in the pocket of my coat, which was behind the DJ stand. There was no way to leave. My face was covered with mace pepper spray and before I knew it I was staring at a gun being pointed at me. I was too afraid to move, and I thought my life was over, BUT God.

Although I experienced that, it still was not enough to get me to come in from the nightclub. There are times when God tries to send warnings before destruction, but we ignore the warnings. As a dreamer, I saw the devastation and I knew I needed to change. This was God's way of turning my life around, again making me right in His eyes. So, I went from the nightclub to the church. My past followed me to the church, and I was not able to separate who I was from who God has ordained me to be, but I kept going to the church. Rejected by the church, but I kept going. God saved me so many times, and I felt like I owed it to Him to give Him my life. That meant that I had to forget about Tasha and think more about Jesus.

My Wrong Made Right

My wrongs are right because of God. God forgave me for everything I have done in my past. When I look back over my life and see where the Lord has brought me from, all I can do is say, "Thank you, Lord," for making me right with you. The scripture says, in Romans 3:23–24, "*For everyone has sinned; we all fall short of God's glorious standards. Yet*

God, in his grace, freely makes us right in his sight. He did this through Christ Jesus when he freed us from the penalty for our sins."

The grace of God is for everyone. Let not your heart feel troubled about the things of the past, but trust in the Lord and all that He has said concerning you. You are not your mistake, nor are you stuck because of past failures. When the Bible says we have all fallen short of the glory of God; that means even the Apostles made mistakes. Just because they made mistakes it did not stop God from using them for His glory. Ask the Lord to forgive you for your sins and move forward toward your purpose. Do not stay where you are because you do not feel that you deserve to preach the Word of God. God has already gone before you and moved every wrong that you have done and destroyed it. Forget about it and know that you are made right in the sight of the Lord.

No matter what you have done, if you ask Him to forgive you and mean it with your whole heart, you can rest in knowing that you have been set free. All the times I did not do everything right, God made it right. When I drank too much, God cleaned my body and made it all right. The time I was sleeping with a man who was not my husband, God forgave me and made it right by sending me a loving husband. When I thought it was money that helped me get where I am today, God fixed my mind and showed me that

I am who I am because He made it right. The time I hated myself and my life, God made it right by letting me know that He has given me life and life more abundantly. All I can say is that I am forgiven, set free, made whole, healed from my past, loved, intelligent, and successful all because God made my wrongs right!

Author Dr. Natasha Bibbins

Natasha Bibbins is a God-fearing woman who loves the Lord and her family. She is a Wife, Mother, Evangelist, Prophetess, Co-Author, Author, Certified Life & Executive Leadership Coach, Sister, and a Friend. She received an Honorary Doctorate degree from the School of Great Commission Bible College – Eastern Shore Campus by Dean Dr. Francis Bailey. She is the founder of Natasha Bibbins Ministries Forever Fire Empowerment (501C3), Sisters Empowering Sisters Ministries, and The ReCharge Movement, all birthed under Natasha Bibbins Ministries. As a child, she grew up in church but did not accept God into her life until she was a teenager, after the sudden death of her brother. Even after accepting Christ, she still ran from her calling due to fear.

After running for so many years, she finally gave God a real "yes" and lived *totally* for God in 2012. She became a minister-in-training for more than five years, prior to being ordained in 2018. As an MIT she learned the importance of how to "follow the leader" to prepare her for ministry and she also received a certificate in Bible Studies from Christian Leaders Institute. She used all the skills she developed to assist her with Intercessory Prayer Ministry, where she learned the importance of prayer and intercession.

Natasha joined The FOCUS Accelerator mentoring group in 2022 to prepare her for The Christian Leadership Coaching program, a program that would train and develop the leaders of the church. Natasha was a part of the Glory Mentorship Program in 2018 where she learned how to operate fully in her God-given gifts.

She is the visionary of The Walker Family Prayer Call as she believes in the principle that family is her first ministry as spoken in 1 Timothy 3:5: "If anyone does not know how to manage his own family, how can he take care of God's church?"

Natasha also became a best-selling co-author in 2020 for the *Dreamer on the Rise* book and again in 2022 for her *Called to Intercede* book. She is also the author of *ReCharge Empowerment and Journal.* She believes that knowledge and wisdom are the keys to being effective in any ministry. Just as Daniel had to be trained for three years before he could enter royal service in Daniel 1:5, so shall she go through the training process. Natasha was honored with two awards, a Servant Leader Award and Walking in Grace Leadership

Award in 2022.

Professionally, Natasha has a master's degree in Management, a bachelor's degree in Business Management, and an associate degree in Business Administration. She is currently a student at Liberty University, in pursuit of her Doctor of Strategic Leadership degree.

Natasha is married to Michael Bibbins, and is the birth mother of two children, Wilniqua and William Battle. Natasha is blessed to have three Bonus Children: Michael II, Shenelle, and Pamela. She is also blessed to have one beautiful granddaughter named Aniya and one son-in-love, Harold Goethe.

Natasha's favorite scripture is Romans 8:18: "*For I reckon that the sufferings of this present time are not worthy to be compared to the glory which shall be revealed in us.*" This scripture reminds her to keep pressing and keep pushing because greatness is right around the corner.

Amen.

Contact Information:

Facebook: Natasha Bibbins
Facebook: Sisters Empowering Sisters
Facebook: Recharge
Facebook: Forever Fire Empowerment
YouTube: Natasha Bibbins

Instagram: natasha_t_bibbins

Email: admini@natashabibbins.com

Email: natashabibbinsministries@gmail.com

Website: www.natashabibbins.com

Natasha's Acknowledgements

I would like to first thank God for all that He has done in my life. This is not a cliché because when I think about all the things God has done for me, all the ways He made for me, all the things He protected me from, ALL I can do is Thank Him. I would like to thank my husband and my best friend, Mr. Michael Bibbins, for your patience, support, and unselfish love throughout this entire journey. Thank you for always encouraging me to be better. Your famous words to me are always "Be the best version of you" and for that I am truly GRATEFUL that God allowed you to be my husband. The Bible says in Proverbs 18:22 (KJV) that, "*Whoso findeth a wife findeth a good thing, and obtaineth favour from the Lord.*" I thank God for choosing me to be your FAVOR!

I would like to thank my children, William and Wilniqua Battle, who have always been the reason why I strived to be better and better every day. I would like to thank all my family and friends that have supported and loved me. Lastly, I would like to thank every person who has supported my ministries through the years. You all will never know how much it means to me to have you in my life.

I remember a trusted voice stated, "*A leader without any followers would be someone taking a lonely walk.*" Thank you all for not allowing me to walk alone. I love you all!